GR8

*Steps for new Christians
(aged 7¾ -11)*

by Sammy Horner

CHRISTIAN FOCUS PUBLICATIONS

WHAT'S INSIDE...

Published by Christian Focus Publications Ltd
Geanies House, Tain, Ross-shire, IV20 1TW
© 1997 Sammy Horner
Illustrations by Tim Charnick, Profile Design

ISBN 1-85792-231-X

WHAT'S IT ALL ABOUT?

So you've become a Christian!
There will be lots of things that you
will want to know about and understand,
and this little book is a great place to start!

Have a great time learning and
growing as a Christian...read on!

PS: If you don't understand some of the words that are used,
remember to look at the back of the book for an explanation!

IT'S LIFE - BUT NOT AS WE KNOW IT

When you took the step of becoming a Christian, you started on a new way of life...living like Jesus!

Deciding to follow Jesus means that we have realised that we have been living the wrong way - our own way! Without God's love and forgiveness we cannot live as he intended us to.

Jesus loved his Father, and now that you have decided to follow him, your actions and thoughts towards God will also begin to change as you get to know him more.

Loving God with all that we have is the most important lesson that we can learn. But now that you are a Christian, you must also learn to love and care for others as well, (Jesus said that loving other people was the second most important thing that anyone can learn!).

Being a Christian means that you have started to have the best relationship that anyone could ever have!

THINK BEFORE YOU READ ON...
How did God begin to speak to you?

Was it through:

Maybe God began to show how much he cared for you by some other brilliant way? God is not limited in how he speaks to us - it's important that we listen to what he says.

BABIES NEED FOOD

Just as your body
needs food to keep
it strong and healthy,
so the new life you
now have needs
a good balanced
diet. If you are going
to grow into a strong
Christian, you need to be fed!

God has given us a very special book, called the
Bible which is full of good things which will help
you to grow.

Milk is the food for babies.
Did you know that some
parts of the Bible are
described as milk for
new Christians?
These are the
best places to
start reading.

GOOD FOOD FOR NEW CHRISTIANS

The Bible is a big book to read, so don't be put off by the size of it!

It begins with the story of God's amazing creation of the world. However, things go wrong when people start to disobey God and please themselves.

As a result, all people have been separated from God because of sin.

But it also tells us about God's great rescue plan. He has made it possible for everyone to become his friend if they want to - something you have just discovered!

The first part of the Bible is called the Old Testament and is actually made up of 39 separate 'books'. To begin your Bible adventure, turn over the page to find a good starting place...

SOME MILKY BITS...

Great stories which are easier to understand.

Where they're found in the Bible
(if you have difficulty finding these books, look up the contents page)

The Creation
Genesis : chapters 1-2

The Big Flood
Genesis : chapters 6-8

The Commands of God
Exodus : chapter 20 verses 1-17

The story of David
1 Samuel: chapters 16-31
2 Samuel: chapters 1-24

SOME MEATY BITS...

More great stories, which contain some harder bits to understand.

Joshua
The book of Joshua

Daniel
The book of Daniel

The books called:
Leviticus
Numbers
1 & 2 Chronicles

The second part of the Bible is called the New Testament and is made up of 27 books, (although some of them are actually short letters).

The New Testament talks a lot about a very special person - Jesus. The first 4 books are called the Gospels and they tell us who Jesus is, what he has done and what that means for us.

MILKY BITS

The stories about Jesus.
Stories that Jesus told.
Both found in the books:
Matthew, Mark, Luke and
John.

The beginning of the
book called Acts.

MEATY BITS

The book called **Romans**
The book called **Hebrews**
The book called **James**

There are loads of other books in the Bible, these
are just ideas to get you started.

As you start reading you'll soon see that
there are some bits of the Bible that are more
difficult to understand than others. As you 'grow
up' you will be able to understand more of the
meaty bits, but don't worry if it takes time! The
important thing is to get the 'food' that you need.

*As well as the Bible, you can get special videos, games,
activity packs, CDs, tapes, stories and songs that will
nourish you. Ask someone who has been a Christian for
a while if they could find out about things that might help
you! * (See page 29 for more details)*

B ABIES NEED A FAMILY

All babies need someone older to look after them. It is usually a family's job to take care of the newest member. Mum, dad, brothers, sisters granny,grandpa..... even aunts,uncles and cousins often help to look after a new arrival.

The Bible tells us that the people who are called the Church should be like a good family to us.

A church will be made up of old and young people, clever and not so clever. Tall, short, thin, not so thin, men, women, boys, girls, people who have white skin, people who have black skin, brown skin, cool clothes, scruffy clothes, people who can walk and people who can't: in fact, *all kinds of people!*

What everyone of them should have in common is that they love Jesus and do their best to do what he says.

Remember though, just like any family, you may not always agree with everyone at church, and you can say 'No!' to anything that you think might be wrong.

Check first in the Bible to see if what people say or do matches up with the Bible's teaching. If you don't understand something then ask questions... If answers don't make sense to you then say so!

BABIES NEED CLEANED UP!

Babies make an awful mess! They spill things, they get food all over their faces and we won't go into the reason that they wear nappies!

Babies make silly mistakes all the time but it's the only way that they can grow and learn. Some mistakes are things that they cannot help, but they soon learn to stop doing those things.

Other mistakes are made because of bad behaviour. We all grow and learn by making mistakes but doing things wrong on purpose will stop us from growing up healthily. When we do make a mess, we need to learn to say sorry to God and to the people we've hurt.

13

BABIES HAVE THEIR OWN LANGUAGE

Parents love to hear their baby gurgle and laugh! It doesn't make any sense to anyone else, but it is the best sound in the world to a loving parent!

Talking to our heavenly Father is called prayer. You might have heard an older Christian praying and using very big strange words...don't worry! You don't need to talk like that.

God wants you to use your own words when you speak to him.

HOW DO I PRAY?

You can pray anywhere, anytime!

You can pray out loud or quietly, (God even knows what we think!).

14

You can thank God,

ask him to help you,

say you're sorry for
things you've done,

tell him
what makes you angry,
sad, happy or upset.

You can pray for others, but best of all,
the fact that we can pray means that we
can talk to God our friend!
God loves you, and sees you as a special,
valued, wonderful person...

God loves you!

THE TALK AND
THE WALK

Jesus said that it was important to go and tell people the good news about what he wants to do for them. How do you think people might react if you start talking about your faith every time that you meet them?

Does what you say and what you do match up? If the most important thing is to love God first and then other people, are you showing that kind of love?

Will you continue to love someone even if they don't like what you believe...or even if they don't like you?

The Bible says that if we say that we believe in Jesus, but don't try to live like him, then it's like not having 'new life' at all.

Jesus certainly told people about the love of God, but he also...well...check this out!

JESUS...

Spent time with children.

Treated women with great respect.

Allowed the sick to touch him.

Spent time with poor people.

Made friends
with people
who had no friends.

Was never horrible
to people because they
had a different religion,
looked different, or had
different coloured skin.

Spoke up for people
who found themselves
in trouble...

Jesus lived out everything that he believed...that's why they called him, 'The friend of sinners'.

It's important that you share your faith, but you have to show love and respect for other people, no matter how they might respond to what you have to say about Jesus.

YOU'RE NEVER ALONE WHEN YOU'RE ON YOUR OWN

Even when we are on our own, we need to remember that God is still with us. If we are sad or happy, lonely or feeling misunderstood, God has promised to be with us at all times!

If your friends or family make fun of you for becoming a Christian, remember you're not alone - Jesus knew what it felt like to have a hard time.

When doubts or fears try to destroy your new joy and faith, take some of God's promises to heart.

Check out some of the things that he has said...

'No one will take you out of my hand.'

John chapter 10 verse 28

'I will never leave you.'

Hebrews chapter 13 verse 5

Proverbs chapter 18 verse 24

'I will stick closer than a brother.'

Although we can't see Jesus here with us, he promised that he would send his Holy Spirit to be our helper. When we ask Jesus to forgive us and take control of our lives, it is the Holy Spirit who comes and lives inside us.

This promise is amazing! It means that we don't have to count on how we *feel*, but can rely on God's faithfulness.

UNDER PRESSURE...

It was the summer
holidays and
Harry, Yuk and
Snot went *every-*
where together,
they were closer
than a goldfish's eyes!

Yuk was called Yuk because, apart from burgers, fries and sweet things, he hated any other kind of food.

'Fancy some soup?' his mum would say.

'Yuk!' said Yuk.

'How about some nice chicken curry?'

'Yuk!'

'Stew?'

'Yuk!'...and so on! Harry thought that Yuk was cool. 'I wish I could be like Yuk,' he thought.

Snot was completely different from Yuk! Some people thought that he was called Snot because he never carried a hanky, but that was only part of the reason! Snot always thought that *he* knew what was best. If mum told him that it was long past his bed time, Snot would say, 'S'not!'

Harry thought that Snot was excellent, 'I wish I was as smart as Snot!' he thought.

Harry was called Harry because he was called Harry. Harry usually ate all his meals, and went to bed when he was asked to, but he felt like he was really ordinary...nothing special...a bit boring...well, he didn't even have a cool name like Snot!

PRESSURE...PRESSURE...

Yuk always got the best kind of trainers to wear, but Harry had to make do with cheaper ones, just because his dad didn't have a job.

Snot didn't even have a dad, but he still wore better trainers than Harry, and worst of all, sometimes Yuk and Snot would joke about Harry's affordable footwear!

'Right! That's it!', thought Harry, 'if Snot and Yuk can have cool names so can I! If Yuk and Snot can get good trainers, so can I! No one's gonna joke about me anymore...first I need a name!'

Harry thought for ages, 'I've got it ,'Bogie,' Naaa! Too much like Snot! Hmmm...what about 'Belch' or, 'Ugh!' Wait a minute...I've got it...'Finknot'...that's it, I am gonna be Finknot!'

The first job was to get rid of the terrible trainers; it was time to have a word with Mum and Dad!

Harry picked up the sports shoes and headed off to the living room.

'Hi Harry! What are you up to ?' yelled Dad.

'Don't call me Harry!' said Harry, 'everyone calls me Finknot.'

'Finknot...since when?' asked Mum.

'Ummm...For a while now, anyway never mind that, just look at these trainers!'

Harry's mum and dad looked.

'What about them?' said Dad.

'Are they letting water in?' whined Mum.

Harry's face went pink. 'No!' He yelled, 'Look at them...just look at them!'

UNDER PRESSURE...

Both parents looked.
Harry could feel himself getting more and more frustrated.

'You just don't get it do you! Who has ever heard of 'Kiddywinkle' trainers...it's the name... I don't want to wear 'Kiddywinkle' trainers!'

'Well then what *do* you want?' both parents asked in stereo.

'I want Super Pumperama Lazerdisc Urban Street Feet Trainers!'

Harry could see that Mum looked sad. 'We can't afford those kind of shoes Harry. I'm sorry, but you will just need to wear the ones that you have for the time being.'

Harry got ready to use his new name.

'I Finknot!' he yapped, 'you will just need to get me the ones that I want...or else!'

'Yes!' said Dad, 'Or else change your name to 'Finkagain'.'

Mum giggled. Harry didn't. For days Harry grumped around the house, only speaking to his mum and dad when he really had to. 'I'll teach 'em' he thought.

'Tomato soup for lunch!' shouted Dad.

'Finknot!' said Harry who would not touch a drop!

'It's bed time !' cried Mum.

PRESSURE...PRESSURE...

'Finknot' growled Harry as he kept reading his comics.

For days it went on but Harry was *not* going to leave the house in those trainers. After a whole week, Harry was miserable. 'Alright Harry, let's get this sorted out once and for all!' said Dad.

'Finknot!' said Harry quietly.

'Finkagain!' said Dad. This time no one giggled! 'You need to tell me why you are behaving this way Harry. It's causing problems for everyone, not just you!' Harry frowned.

'Why can't I have the new trainers? They don't cost all that much, and you can always afford to put money into the church's collection plate and stuff like that!'

'So that's it!' said Dad. 'Harry you need to understand that Mum and I need to use our money in the best way that we can. We need to pay for our house, our fuel bills, our food, and our clothes. The money we give to church is just as important as any of the other things that we do!'

'Why?' said Harry, 'church is just boring!' Dad sat down on the edge of Harry's bed.

'The little bit of money we give to the church is used in all kinds of different ways. There are practical things needing to be paid for, like heating the building, so that you and I don't freeze on Sunday mornings! How do you think all the games for your club are paid for? The church also helps to send people to work with children who have much less than us!'

UNDER...PRESSURE...

Harry's eyes widened, 'You mean there are other kids who have worse trainers than me?'

His dad smiled, but still looked serious. 'Harry, some children have no parents, no home, no medicine, no food and even no clean water!'

Harry felt bad! Still, what was he going to do? He couldn't back down and he still wanted to have a cool name. Just as his dad left the room, Harry had a brainwave. He got his brightest coloured model paints and painted a big blue line right across the word 'Kiddywinkle'. It looked neat! A red squiggle, a green circle and a big yellow star began to appear on the hated trainers! Within an hour the shoes where dry and on Harry's feet and were carrying him right down to Snot's house.

Snot's mum opened the door.

'Hello Harry!' she smiled. 'Haven't seen you for a while.'

Just then Snot and Yuk came bounding down the stairs...both of them stared at Harry's wildly coloured shoes.

'Where did you get those trainers?' they both yelled.

PRESSURE...PRESSURE...

'Yeah', continued Snot, 'They're cooler than a penguin's bottom!'

'Wish I had a pair' said Yuk, 'how come you always manage to be different Harry?'

'The name is Finkabout!' said Harry.

'Finkabout!' squealed his mates, 'why Finkabout?'

Harry smiled, 'Because from today, I began to Finkabout how special I am and all the things that I have. I realised that trying to be like you guys just makes me miserable, because I'm different. I've had to Finkabout others who don't have nearly as much as me, and that made me Finkabout how selfish I can be. The most important thing I've had to Finkabout is that people need to see the real me! I'm not going to try to be like you Snot, or you Yuk...that just makes everybody miserable!'

The three pals wandered off towards the park laughing and joking.

Finkabout was first to run for the old swings,and just before Snot and Yuk followed, Snot whispered, 'I wish I was as smart as Harry!'

'Yeah!' said Yuk, 'and I wish that I could have cool trainers like his, I mean just look at these old things I've got...Yuk!

UNDER PRESSURE...

It can be hard to feel happy with the way that we are. Sometimes our friends put us under pressure to do and say things that we wouldn't normally do. It's possible that sometimes they don't even mean it! But it is important that we know when we are being pressurised.

If you are asked to do something which is wrong, have the guts to say 'No!' Remember, you can pray for help at any time!

The Bible tells us that we need to learn to be content with the good things that we already have. Wanting what other people have usually makes us want even more!

FRUIT - NOT SOUR GRAPES!

It's a well known fact that fruit is good for you! Fruit is the proof that a tree or a plant is strong and healthy.

The Bible tells us that a growing Christian should also have proof that he or she is healthy in their faith! Yep! We need to bear fruit! Don't panic...you don't need to have bananas growing out of your nose.

Just as milk was a way to describe the simple, but important parts of the Bible, so fruit has another meaning!

The Bible tells us that the fruit that we bear shows others that we are living like Jesus...it is proof that we have the new life that he promised us!

Are you an impatient person normally? Well, the Bible says that *patience* is some of the fruit that a Christian should have!

Are there people that you really hate? The fruit of this new life should be replacing that hate with love!

In the Bible in the book called Galatians, chapter 5, verses 22 and 23 you will find there are 9 fruits mentioned. These are all called the fruit of the Spirit, which means that we are showing qualities as a result of the Holy Spirit living within us.

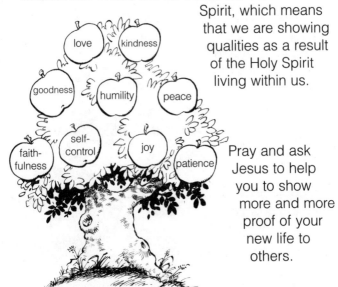

love   kindness
goodness   humility   peace
faith-fulness   self-control   joy   patience

Pray and ask Jesus to help you to show more and more proof of your new life to others.

FOREVER FRIENDS

God has promised to always be our closest friend... absolutely nothing can change that!

He will always love us and never leave us. Even when our bodies die, our friendship with God will not end. He promises us that he will have a special place, called Heaven for us to go to, and we will be with him forever.

_____

You may find the following material
will help you to grow up...

MUSIC: by Sammy Horner & The Wonderkids

Obey the Maker's Instructions	- Rock n' Roll version of the Commandments.
Country Parables	-Country music version of Jesus' stories
The Beatitudes	- Blues music based on Jesus' teaching in Matthew 5

If the above tapes and CD's are not available from your local Christian bookshop, ask them to order a copy for you. If you are unsure where to find the bookshop, ask another Christian to help you.

PARDON ME?

As you grow up in your faith you may come across some strange new words and ideas. To help you understand their meaning we've tried to explain them...

BIBLE - The special book that God has given us. He told lots of different people who believed in him to write down, laws, stories about history, the words of Jesus and the story about how the Church began, (plus loads of other stuff). The Bible tells us what we need to know about men and women, God, Jesus, how we should live, looking after the planet, issues like caring for others and tons more. The Bible is also called God's Word or Scripture.

BORN AGAIN - When we decide to follow Jesus he promises us a new life. The beginning of that new life is like being born again. A chance to start again and have a whole new way of thinking and living...but it's just the start!

CHRISTIAN - Any person of any age who loves Jesus and obeys what Jesus taught.

CHURCH -The name given to all the people who believe in Jesus no matter where they might live in the world.

CREATOR - Another name for God, 'cause he made everything!

FAITH - Being able to believe in God without actually having ever seen him! It can also mean this is what we believe as Christians.

FRUIT - Proof that we are living like Jesus.

GOD - God is everywhere, and he knows everything and sees everything. God is Love, God is good, he is fair, and the most powerful person anywhere!

GOSPEL - This is the Good News about Jesus and every thing that he has done for us and all that he wants to do for us, and how we can get involved.

HEAVEN - A special place that God has made. We know that when our bodies die, we will go there to be with God forever. Heaven is a wonderful place where people won't be sad or unhappy.

HEAVENLY FATHER -One of the names that we can call God. Jesus tells us that our Heavenly Father is always good to us and knows what we need, so no matter how good or bad our normal dad might be, God is always even better.

JESUS - This is the name that was given to God's Son. Jesus means 'Saviour'. Jesus is God in human form.

LORD - Another name we can call Jesus. The Lord is someone who is in control of everything, and is wise and fair.

LOVE - Love doesn't just mean that you go all silly every time you see that cute girl or handsome boy in your class. The Bible says that God is Love! God's love is limitless. He loves people no matter how rotten they might be.

MILK - The important things that we need to know about our faith, that are simple to understand when we are new Christians.

NEW LIFE - What you have after you are born again!

PRAYER - Our way of talking with God about anything at all!

SINNER - The bible says that *every* person who ever lived is a sinner, (except Jesus). We sin when we disobey God.

SPEAK - When we talk about God 'speaking' to us we mean that we have read the Bible and really understood something that God wants us to do. God might also keep reminding you of things that are wrong or need to be changed by showing you things on TV, in books or magazines or by what someone might say to you.

SPIRIT - The Bible talks about God's Spirit or the Holy Spirit. The Holy Spirit is God, and he came to us after Jesus went to heaven. He gives us our new life and helps us understand what he wants us to do for him.

It's exciting to see a baby take their first few steps. Steps lead on to walking, jumping, running...action!

Growing involves learning new things, taking risks and being able to change your mind. God wants his children to grow up to be strong and useful and to love him. Keep growing!